WELCOME TO MY COUNTRY

Welcome to
SAUDI ARABIA

Gareth Stevens Publishing
A WORLD ALMANAC EDUCATION GROUP COMPANY

Written by
GRAEME CANE/DYNISE BALCAVAGE

Edited in USA by
CHRISTINE HEILMAN

Designed by
GEOSLYN LIM

Picture research by
SUSAN JANE MANUEL

First published in North America in 2002 by
Gareth Stevens Publishing
A World Almanac Education Group Company
330 West Olive Street, Suite 100
Milwaukee, Wisconsin 53212 USA

Please visit our web site at:
www.garethstevens.com
For a free color catalog describing
Gareth Stevens Publishing's list of high-quality books
and multimedia programs, call
1-800-542-2595 or
fax your request to (414) 332-3567.

© **TIMES MEDIA PRIVATE LIMITED 2002**
Originated and designed by
Times Editions
an imprint of Times Media Private Limited
Times Centre, 1 New Industrial Road
Singapore 536196
http://www.timesone.com.sg/te

Library of Congress Cataloging-in-Publication Data
Cane, Graeme.
Welcome to Saudi Arabia / Graeme Cane and Dynise Balcavage.
p. cm. — (Welcome to my country)
Summary: Presents information on the geography, history, government
and economy, arts, people, and social life and customs of
Saudi Arabia, the largest country in the Middle East.
Includes bibliographical references and index.
ISBN 0-8368-2538-1 (lib. bdg.)
1. Saudi Arabia—Juvenile literature. [1. Saudi Arabia.]
I. Balcavage, Dynise. II. Title. III. Series.
DS204.25.C36   2002
953.8—dc21   2001057803

Printed in Malaysia

1 2 3 4 5 6 7 8 9 06 05 04 03 02

PICTURE CREDITS
Archive Photos: 37
Art Directors and Trip Photo Library:
    3 (bottom), 5, 6, 7, 9, 12, 14, 18, 20,
    22 (bottom), 23 (both), 24, 26, 27, 28,
    30 (bottom), 33, 40, 41, 44 (both)
Camera Press Ltd.: 10, 15 (center),
    15 (bottom), 16, 17, 34, 36, 38
HBL Network Photo Agency: 3 (center),
    30 (top), 39
Hulton Getty/Archive Photos: 13
The Hutchison Library: cover, 1, 2, 3 (top),
    4, 11, 19, 22 (top), 32, 43, 45
Christine Osborne Pictures: 8, 21, 25, 35
Royal Embassy of Saudi Arabia:
    15 (top), 31

Digital Scanning by Superskill Graphics Pte Ltd

Contents

Words that appear in the glossary are printed in **boldface** type the first time they occur in the text.

Welcome to Saudi Arabia!

Saudi Arabia is a land of kings, camels, palm trees, and oil wells. It is also the birthplace of Islam, one of the world's great religions. Each year, thousands of **Muslims** visit the holy cities of Mecca and Medina. Let's learn more about this desert kingdom and its people.

Opposite: This clock tower in Riyadh displays Saudi Arabia's emblem — two crossed swords under a palm tree.

Below: Like all citizens of Saudi Arabia, these boys are Muslims.

The Flag of Saudi Arabia

Saudi Arabia's flag, adopted in 1973, has two white images on an emerald green background. The Arabic words at the top mean "There is no God but Allah, and Muhammad is His Prophet." Below these words is a sword.

The Land

With an area of about 829,000 square miles (2,147,110 square kilometers), Saudi Arabia is only one-fourth the size of the United States, yet it is the largest country in the Middle East. Its western coast is on the Red Sea. The Persian Gulf, as well as the countries of Qatar, Bahrain, and the United Arab Emirates, are to the east. Oman and Yemen are to the south. Jordan, Iraq, and Kuwait are to the north.

Below:
A gravel desert meets a sand desert in western Saudi Arabia.

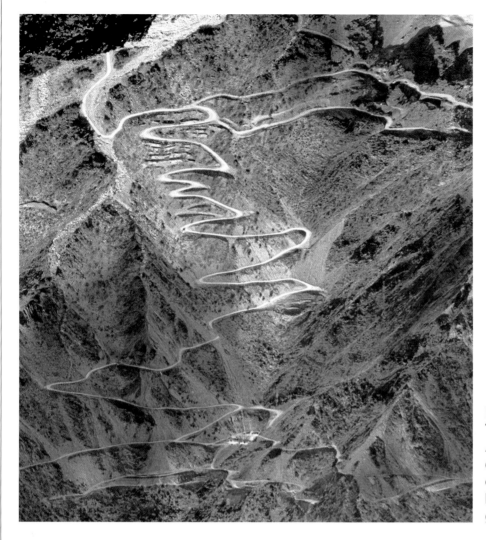

Left:
The mountainous Asir province is called "the garden of Saudi Arabia" because of its green landscape.

Although the southwest has some spectacular mountains, most of Saudi Arabia is desert. About half of it is the *Rub Al-Khali* (roob ahl-HAH-lee), or Empty Quarter, the world's largest sand desert. The An-Nafud desert is in the north. The Eastern Province has salt flats, or *sabkha* (SOB-hah).

Climate

Saudi Arabia is one of the world's driest countries. Most areas get less than 5 inches (127 millimeters) of rain in a year, and parts of the desert might not get any rain for ten years. In summer, temperatures are as high as 120° Fahrenheit (49° Celsius), and strong winds cause sandstorms. Winters are cool. Temperatures in the north may even drop below freezing.

Water is scarce in a country as dry as Saudi Arabia. Underground wells supply some fresh water, but finding

Below: Saudi Arabia's salt flats were formed when water evaporated from salt lakes, mostly in the Ash Sharqiyah province.

Left:
Camels have been important animals in Saudi Arabia for about four thousand years. Not only do they carry people and goods across the desert, but they also provide nutritious milk.

enough water for everyone is difficult. The government has special factories that remove salt from seawater to make it suitable for drinking and bathing.

Plants and Animals

A surprising number of plants and animals thrive in the desert. Where scarlet pimpernel, desert chamomile, and wild iris can grow, however, only one percent of the land can be used for farming. Animals include **ibex**, **oryx**, hyenas, rabbits, scorpions, and cobras.

History

The desert climate of Saudi Arabia shaped the lives of its earliest people. More than three thousand years ago, **nomads** roamed the deserts with their herds of sheep and goats. Later, people of the Saba' kingdom settled near **oases** in the southwestern part of the country and grew crops. The Sabaeans built dams to **irrigate** their fields.

Below: Nabataeans built cave tombs at Madain Saleh two thousand years ago.

The Nabataeans were early settlers in northwestern Saudi Arabia. They are known for carving beautiful cities out of cliffs and rocks.

Many people of the early kingdoms were merchants who earned a living trading silk, ivory, gold, animal skins, and spices such as **frankincense** and **myrrh**. Cities grew along their trade routes. Two of the cities were Mecca and Medina.

Above:
The seventeenth-century palace of Ibn Madi is in the Najran province, which is famous for its ancient castles and watch towers.

Islam

The prophet Muhammad was born in Mecca in A.D. 570. He founded Islam in Medina in 622 and soon **converted** the people of Mecca. As Islam spread to Spain, India, and central Asia, Mecca became the center of a Muslim empire.

By 750, however, warfare among Arab tribes had divided the country, and in the 1500s, the Ottoman Turks conquered some of the western areas. In the 1700s, a religious leader named Abd Al-Wahhab encouraged Arabians to unite by returning to the original teachings of the prophet Muhammad.

The Wahhabi movement helped bring Arabian tribes back together, but the country was not united again until 1932, when Abdul Aziz Ibn Saud drove out the Turks and became king.

Left: Muhammad Ibn Saud, a member of the powerful Al-Saud tribe, helped lead the Wahhabi movement in the mid-1700s.

The Royal Kingdom

Since 1932, members of Ibn Saud's family have ruled Saudi Arabia. When Ibn Saud died in 1953, his son Saud became king. In 1964, Saud's brother Faisal replaced him. During his reign, King Faisal worked hard to modernize Saudi Arabia. Today, it is one of the world's richest countries.

Above: Crown Prince Abdullah Bin Abdul Aziz is next in line to the throne.

King Faisal was **assassinated** in 1975, so his half-brother Khalid took the throne. When Khalid died, in 1982, the present king, Fahd, became ruler. Fahd is known for his good business sense and his interest in developing friendships with Western countries.

King Fahd helped form the *Majlis Al-Shura* (MITE-jlees ahl-SHOE-rah), a council that discusses the concerns of the Saudi Arabian people. Fahd has also enlarged the **mosques** in Mecca and Medina so that Muslims from all over the world can come to worship in these holy cities.

King Abdul Aziz Ibn Saud (c. 1880–1953)

In 1902, young Prince Abdul Aziz Ibn Saud conquered Riyadh. By 1932, he had taken over the entire country and established the new kingdom of Saudi Arabia.

King Abdul Aziz Ibn Saud

King Faisal (c. 1906–1975)

Faisal Bin Abdul Aziz modernized Saudi Arabia, and the country prospered under his rule. He also built good relationships with foreign countries and other Islamic nations.

King Faisal

King Fahd (1923–)

Saudi Arabia's present king, Fahd Bin Abdul Aziz, has strengthened the country's economy, and he has improved ties with Western nations. Due to poor health in recent years, King Fahd has handed over many of his duties to Prince Abdullah.

King Fahd

Government and the Economy

Saudi Arabia is ruled by a king, who must be a member of the royal family. The princes of the royal family choose the king, but the *ulema* (oo-leh-MAH), a group of Muslim religious leaders, must approve their choice. The king appoints a Council of Ministers to help him run the government.

Left: King Fahd's palace in Riyadh has features of traditional Arab architecture, such as windows that are shaped like keyholes.

Each of Saudi Arabia's thirteen provinces has a governor appointed by the king. Saudi people can attend special meetings, called *majlis* (MITE-jlees), to discuss issues or complaints against the government with their local officials, or even with the king.

Above: Criminals in Saudi Arabia are punished in public to discourage other people from breaking the law.

The king runs the country according to Islamic law, and the Saudi Arabian justice system has religious courts that enforce the law. Each court has a judge, but no jury. The king himself is the country's highest court.

Oil and Other Industries

With 25 percent of the world's oil reserves, Saudi Arabia is the largest oil producer in the Middle East. Oil makes up 90 percent of the country's exports. Gold, silver, zinc, and natural gas are also among its **resources**.

Products manufactured in Saudi Arabia include iron, cement, electrical equipment, and processed foods.

Above: The world's largest oil refinery is in Saudi Arabia at Ras Tanura, near the Persian Gulf.

Farmers grow wheat, rice, barley, and grapes, and the country is one of the world's largest producers of dates.

The Workforce

Foreign workers are a large part of the Saudi Arabian workforce. People come from all over the world to work as doctors, teachers, engineers, and in other fields. Saudi women are also joining the workforce. Some work for the government, others run businesses.

Below:
Some Saudi Arabian farmers still harvest dates by hand.

People and Lifestyle

Of Saudi Arabia's 22 million people, about 16.5 million are citizens. The rest are from different countries and have different backgrounds. More than 80 percent of the population are Saudi Arabs. Another 10 percent are Arabs from Yemen. About 3 percent are from the Arab countries in Africa and Asia. Still, all Saudis are Muslims, and they all speak the same Arabic language.

Left:
Some houses along the Tihamah coast look like houses in Africa, which is across the Red Sea from Saudi Arabia.

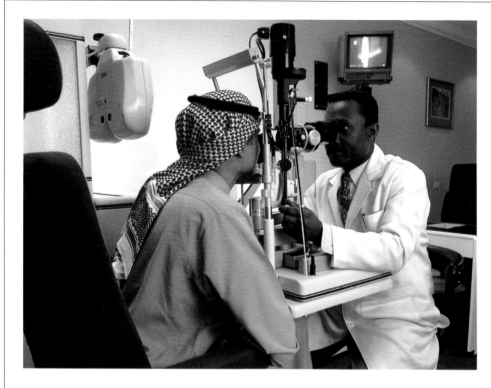

Left: Free health care is available to both citizens and Muslim visitors at Saudi Arabia's modern medical facilities.

Working Life

The Saudi workweek is Saturday to Wednesday. Businesses are closed on Friday, the Muslim holy day, and during daily prayer times. Workdays usually start at 7 a.m. and include a long break in the afternoon.

Health Care

Saudi Arabia has modern hospitals and a high standard of health care. In Riyadh, King Faisal Specialist Hospital is one of the best in the world.

Family Life

Families in Saudi Arabia are usually large, with an average of six or seven children. The oldest male is the head of the family, and all other family members accept his decisions.

Saudis respect and care for older adults, so grandparents, parents, and children often live together in the same house. Traditionally, Islamic men and women live in separate areas of the house, but this custom is gradually changing, especially in the cities.

Dress

Saudi Arabian clothing follows Islamic rules and keeps people comfortable in all kinds of weather. A man wears a long, white robe, or *thobe* (THOBE), and a small cap, or *tagia* (tahj-EE-ah), with a white or red-and-white checked head cloth, called a *gutra* (GOH-trah), over it. An *agal* (ah-GAHL) is a black cord that holds the gutra in place. A woman must wear a long, black gown, called an *abayah* (ah-BYE-ah), and a veil when she is out in public.

Above: According to Islamic law, women must cover their heads and bodies when they are out in public. In some cities, they are expected to cover their faces, too.

Left: This tailor is sewing a *mishlah* (meesh-LAH-hah), which is a cloak worn by Saudi men in cool weather.

23

Education

For Saudi Arabian citizens, education is free, but it is not required. More boys attend school than girls, because many families do not consider an education necessary for girls. Most children start kindergarten at age six, then attend six years of elementary school, three years of middle school, and three years of high school. At all levels, boys and girls go to separate schools, and each class has only about fifteen students.

Below:
As traditional roles in Saudi Arabia change, more women are going to college.

Although the kingdom has eight universities, thousands of Saudi Arabians, especially male students, attend colleges and universities in the United States each year.

To help more adults learn to read and write, Saudi Arabia has created about 2,500 adult education centers. The country's Ministry of Education also runs special schools for people with disabilities.

Above: Classrooms in Saudi Arabia are equipped with the latest technology.

Religion

Islam is the official religion of Saudi Arabia. In fact, it is the only religion allowed in the country, and it is a central part of Saudi Arabia's law, government, and culture.

Approximately 90 percent of the Saudi people are Sunni Muslims. The other 10 percent are Shi'ite Muslims. All Muslims believe in one God, Allah, and in His prophet, Muhammad. They also believe in other prophets known to Christians and Jews, including Jesus.

The **Qur'an** is the holy book of Islam. Muslims believe the Qur'an records the exact words of Allah, which the angel Gabriel told to the prophet Muhammad. Muhammad memorized Allah's message, and **scribes** wrote it down.

In daily life, Muslims observe five basic principles called the pillars of Islam. Five times a day, they must face the city of Mecca to pray, and for the month of **Ramadan**, they must not eat or drink from sunrise to sunset.

Left: Handwritten passages from the Qur'an are carefully handed down from one generation to the next.

Language

Saudi Arabia's official language is Arabic, but English is often spoken in cities. Children study both Arabic and English in school.

Unlike English, Arabic is written from right to left. Its graceful, curling letters are beautiful to look at. About six hundred English words come from the Arabic language, including *sugar*, *caravan*, *cotton*, *giraffe*, and *algebra*.

Below: These schoolboys are enjoying a picture book together.

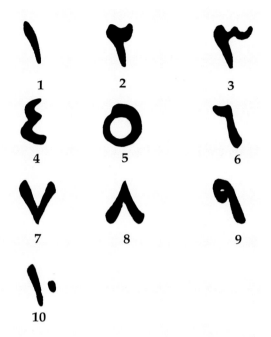

Saudi Arabian television broadcasts in Arabic on one channel and English on another, and three of the country's newspapers are published in English. All publications are **censored** to make sure their contents do not **conflict** with Islamic teachings.

Literature

The Qur'an is the main work of Arabic literature, and, even today, it inspires all Saudi Arabian art forms. A tradition of passing on poems by word of mouth also has continued to the present day.

Arts

Because the Qur'an does not permit Saudi artists to draw people or animals, most designs have **geometric** and floral patterns. Artists also produce beautiful hand lettering, called calligraphy, on paintings, sculpture, metalwork, glass, ceramics, and textiles. The lettering usually forms a quote from the Qur'an.

The **Bedouin** make silver jewelry decorated with amber, coral, turquoise, and pearls. Pieces of jewelry are often shaped like a hand to represent the five pillars of Islam. Some pieces are worn for protection against evil. Weaving is another Bedouin art form.

Above:
This woman's dress and jewelry show the embroidery and silver craftsmanship of the Bedouin.

Opposite: A Saudi artist embroiders the *kiswah* (KEES-wah), which is the cloth that covers the *Kabah* (KAH-bah) in the Grand Mosque at Mecca.

Left:
Bedouin women wear layers of handmade jewelry.

Architecture

Standing side by side with modern architecture, the mosques in Saudi Arabia are some of the country's greatest works of art. Present-day Saudi architects admire traditional Islamic designs and try to create a blend of old and new building styles.

Music and Dance

The rhythms of Middle Eastern music and the instruments used to play it are different from Western music. The *oud* (OOD) is a stringed instrument played like a guitar, the *rebaba* (reh-BAH-bah) is a one-stringed Bedouin instrument, and the *rigg* (REEG) is a tambourine.

Saudi Arabia's national dance, the *ardha* (AHR-dah), is an ancient sword dance performed by men while a poet sings, and drummers keep the beat.

Below: Ardha performances are occasionally held in theaters but are more common at outdoor festivals.

Leisure

In Saudi Arabia, social life follows the laws of Islam, and people spend most of their free time with family members and close friends. Related families often live in groups of houses called compounds, so brothers, sisters, and cousins grow up playing together. The ancient game of *tawle* (tah-LEE), or backgammon, is a favorite pastime.

Below: Especially on cool evenings, Saudi Arabians may use the flat roofs of their houses as places to relax in the open air.

Left: City parks are popular places on a Friday, the Muslim holy day.

Outdoor Activities

Saudi families like to spend time in the kingdom's national parks. They enjoy hiking, picnics, and camping. Some people even go camping in the desert, following the nomadic tradition of their ancestors. Swimmers and divers like to explore the beautiful coral reefs off the Saudi Arabian coast in the Red Sea.

Sports

Soccer is Saudi Arabia's number one sport, but basketball is a close second. Although basketball has been played in Saudi Arabia only since the 1950s, the country, today, has more than thirty club teams. Its national team was first in the 1996 Gulf Championships and 1997 Arab Basketball Championships.

Golf is also a popular sport in Saudi Arabia. Saudis use bright red golf balls because they are easier to see on the sandy desert golf courses.

Above:
Young Saudi soccer players usually get together late in the afternoon, when the Sun is not so strong.

The Saudi government encourages all citizens, especially young people, to participate in sports. Almost every town has a stadium and other sports facilities. In some large towns, the government has built "sports cities" that have huge stadiums, Olympic-size swimming pools, and sports clinics. The kingdom also has more than twenty youth sports camps where young Saudis can train for soccer, basketball, archery, tennis, volleyball, and many other sports.

Below: At the 2000 Olympic Games in Sydney, Australia, Saudi athlete Hadi Souan Somayli won a silver medal in the 400-meter hurdles event.

Traditional Sports

Camel racing, horse racing, and hunting are traditional Saudi sports that are still very popular today. Many Saudis like to watch horse races, even though their religion forbids them to make bets. Some Saudis hunt with a breed of dog called the saluki, and some still train pet falcons to hunt small animals.

Below: The Arabian horse, which is one of the most popular horse breeds in the world, is well-known for its grace and intelligence.

Religious Holidays

Every year, the people of Saudi Arabia celebrate two official Islamic holidays. *Eid Al-Fitr* (EED ahl-feetr) is a three-day festival at the end of Ramadan. During this time, people offer gifts to the poor and enjoy large, festive meals with family and friends. *Eid Al-Adha* (EED ahl-ahd-HAH) is the feast of **sacrifice** during which Muslims kill a lamb or a goat and share the animal's meat with friends, family members, and the poor. It is celebrated at the end of the **hajj**, or **pilgrimage**, to Mecca.

Above:
During Eid Al-Fitr, Muslim families end their Ramadan fasting with a big meal of specially prepared foods.

Food

Saudi Arabian food is flavored with spices such as cardamom, cinnamon, cumin, and coriander. Islamic law forbids Muslims to eat pork, but many dishes are made with lamb or chicken.

At the beginning of a meal, Saudis enjoy appetizers, such as *baba ganoush* (BAH-bah GAH-noozh), a dip made

Left: At mealtime, Saudis usually sit on cushions, on a carpeted floor.

40

from roasted eggplant, and *kibbeh* (KEEB-beh), spicy deep-fried balls of lamb and wheat. *Hasaa al-gareesh* (HAH-sah ahl-gah-REESH), a wheat soup made with lamb, tomatoes, and cinnamon, is a special treat.

Popular main dishes are *mensaf* (MAHN-sahf), which is stewed lamb, and spicy chicken with tomatoes and vegetables. For dessert, Saudis eat dates, either plain or with cream, and pastries filled with nuts and honey.

Above:
Saudi Arabians often use a piece of flat bread called *khboz* (HOH-bohs) to scoop up food.

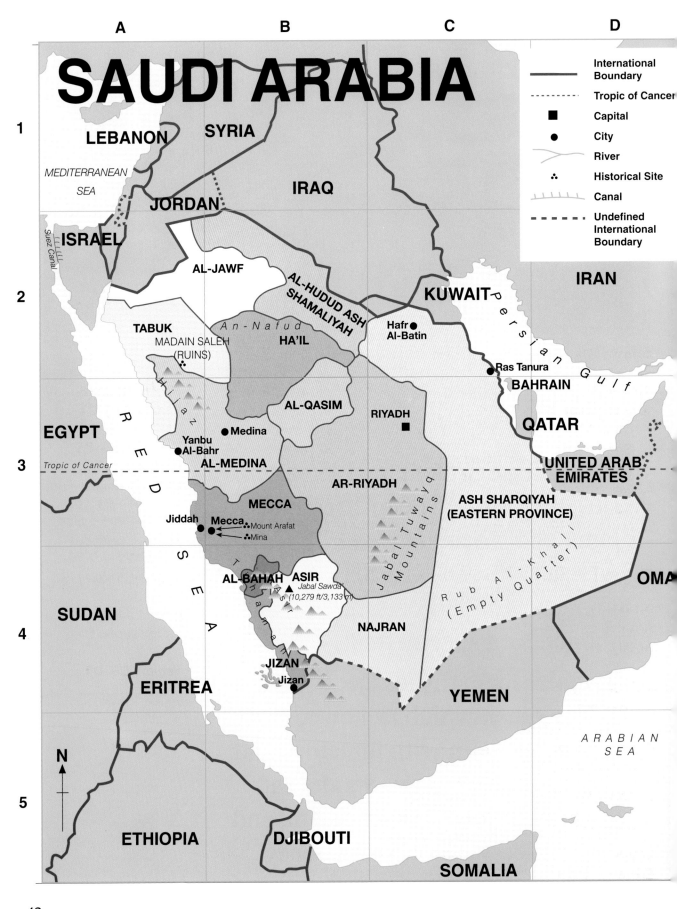

SAUDI ARABIA

Legend:
- International Boundary
- Tropic of Cancer
- Capital ■
- City ●
- River
- Historical Site
- Canal
- Undefined International Boundary

LEBANON
SYRIA
IRAQ
MEDITERRANEAN SEA
JORDAN
ISRAEL
Suez Canal
AL-JAWF
AL-HUDUD ASH SHAMALIYAH
KUWAIT
IRAN
An-Nafud
TABUK
MADAIN SALEH (RUINS)
HA'IL
Hafr Al-Batin
Ras Tanura
Hijaz
RED SEA
BAHRAIN
AL-QASIM
RIYADH
EGYPT
Medina
Yanbu Al-Bahr
AL-MEDINA
QATAR
Tropic of Cancer
AR-RIYADH
UNITED ARAB EMIRATES
MECCA
Jiddah
Mecca
Mount Arafat
Mina
ASH SHARQIYAH (EASTERN PROVINCE)
Jabal Tuwayq Mountains
Rub Al-Khali (Empty Quarter)
AL-BAHAH
ASIR
Jabal Sawda (10,279 ft/3,133 m)
OMAN
Tihama
SUDAN
NAJRAN
JIZAN
Jizan
ERITREA
YEMEN
ARABIAN SEA
N
ETHIOPIA
DJIBOUTI
SOMALIA

Persian Gulf

42

Above: This Saudi family's farm is in the Najran province.

Al-Bahah (province) B4
Al-Hudud ash Shamaliyah (province) B2
Al-Jawf (province) A2–B2
Al-Medina (province) A2–B3
Al-Qasim (province) B2–B3
An-Nafud B2
Arabian Sea D4–D5
Ar-Riyadh (province) B3–C4
Ash Sharqiyah (Eastern Province) B2–D4
Asir (province) B4
Asir Mountains B4

Bahrain C3

Djibouti B5

Egypt A2–A3
Eritrea A4–B5

Ethiopia A5–B5

Ha'il (province) B2–B3
Hijaz Mountains A2–A3

Iran C1–D2
Iraq B1–C2
Israel A1–A2

Jabal Sawda' B4
Jabal Tuwayq Mountains C3–C4
Jiddah A3
Jizan (province) B4
Jordan A2–B1

Kuwait C2

Lebanon A1

Madain Saleh (ruins) A2
Mecca (city) B3
Mecca (province) A3–B4
Medina B3

Mediterranean Sea A1–A2
Mina B3
Mount Arafat B3

Najran (province) B4–C4

Oman D3–D4

Persian Gulf C2–D3

Qatar C3–D3

Ras Tanura C2
Red Sea A2–B5
Riyadh C3

Rub Al-Khali (Empty Quarter) C4–D4

Somalia B5–C5
Sudan A3–A5
Suez Canal A2
Syria A1–B1

Tabuk (province) A2–B3
Tihamah (plain) B4

United Arab Emirates D3

Yemen B5–D4

Quick Facts

Official Name   Kingdom of Saudi Arabia

Capital   Riyadh

Official Language   Arabic

Population   22,757,092 (July 2001 estimate)

Land Area   829,000 square miles (2,147,110 square km)

Provinces   Al-Bahah, Al-Hudud ash Shamaliyah, Al-Jawf, Al-Medina, Al-Qasim, Ar-Riyadh, Ash Sharqiyah (Eastern Province), Asir, Ha'il, Jizan, Mecca, Najran, Tabuk

Type of Government   Monarchy

Government Leader   King Fahd Bin Abdul Aziz

Highest Point   Jabal Sawda' 10,279 feet (3,133 m)

Major Cities   Jiddah, Mecca, Medina, Riyadh

Major Industry   Oil

Official Religion   Islam

Holy Sites   Mecca, Medina

Currency   Saudi riyal (3.75 riyals = U.S. $1, since 1986)

Opposite: A Saudi father and his sons visit the Masmak Fortress in Riyadh.

45

Glossary

assassinated: murdered a government leader or a well-known public figure.

Bedouin: nomadic people who live in the deserts of the Middle East.

censored: examined to remove words or pictures that might be considered unsuitable or offensive.

conflict: go against.

converted: changed beliefs from one religion to another.

frankincense: a sweet-smelling, sticky substance that comes from the trunk of the frankincense tree.

geometric: having shapes such as circles, triangles, and rectangles.

hajj: the pilgrimage to the holy city of Mecca that Muslims try to make at least once in their lifetimes.

ibex: a wild mountain goat with long, curved horns.

irrigate: use ditches or pipes to bring a supply of water to an area of land where crops are planted.

Kabah: a small stone building inside Mecca's Grand Mosque, which holds a black stone that is sacred to Muslims.

mosques: buildings where Muslims go to worship.

Muslims: people who follow the teachings of the Islamic religion.

myrrh: a bitter, sticky, brown substance that comes from the bark of a tree and is used to make perfume and incense.

nomads: desert dwellers with no permanent home, who move from place to place in search of food for themselves and their animals.

oases: places in the desert that have water and where trees and other plants can grow.

oryx: a kind of antelope that roams the deserts of Africa and Saudi Arabia.

pilgrimage: a journey to a holy place to show religious devotion.

Qur'an: the holy book of Islam.

Ramadan: the month in the Islamic year when Muslims do not eat or drink between sunrise and sunset.

resources: the materials a country has to meet the needs of its people or to sell or trade.

sacrifice: the act of offering or giving up something to God as a sign of faith and devotion.

scribes: people who were employed to write down or copy books and documents before printing presses were invented.

More Books to Read

The Arabian Nights Entertainments. Andrew Lang (Dover Publications)

Hosni the Dreamer: An Arabian Tale. Ehud Ben-Ezer (Farrar, Straus and Giroux)

Muslim Festival Tales. Kerena Marchant (Raintree Steck-Vaughn)

Muslim Mosque. Places of Worship series. Angela Wood (Gareth Stevens)

Ramadan. Suhaib Hamid Ghazi (Holiday House)

Rashid of Saudi Arabia. How They Live Now series. Zahra Freeth (Lutterworth)

Saudi Arabia. Faces and Places series. Bob Temple (Child's World)

Saudi Arabia. Festivals of the World series. Maria O'Shea (Gareth Stevens)

Saudi Arabia in Pictures. Visual Geography series. Eugene Gordon (Lerner Publications)

A Ticket to Saudi Arabia. Laurie Halse Anderson (Carolrhoda Books)

Videos

American Cultures for Children: Arab-American Heritage. (Schlessinger Media)

History Makers: Lawrence of Arabia. (Madacy Entertainment)

Holidays for Children: Ramadan. (Schlessinger Media)

World's Last Great Places. Arabia: Sand, Sea and Sky. (National Geographic)

Web Sites

eho.org/kids/saudiarabia.htm

travel.yahoo.com/t/Middle_East/ Saudi_Arabia

www.arab.net/saudi/saudi_contents.html

www.saudiembassy.net/profile/saudi-profile00.htm

Due to the dynamic nature of the Internet, some web sites stay current longer than others. To find additional web sites, use a reliable search engine with one or more of the following keywords to help you locate information on Saudi Arabia. Keywords: *camels, date palms, deserts, hajj, Islam, Mecca, Muhammad, nomads, Ramadan.*

Index